FLORENCE IN THE TIME OF THE MEDICI

E. R. Chamberlin

SAPERE
BOOKS

FLORENCE IN THE TIME OF THE MEDICI

Published by Sapere Books.

20 Windermere Drive, Leeds, England, LS17
7UZ,

United Kingdom

saperebooks.com

ISBN: 978-1-80055-525-9.

TABLE OF CONTENTS

TO THE READER

This book is about a city as it was nearly 500 years ago. It was not particularly large as cities go — indeed, if it could be placed beside, say, London or Manchester or Liverpool as they are today it would seem to be little more than a country town. A citizen could have walked across it in about half-an-hour and, as in any other small town, he would probably have known most of his fellow-citizens by sight. Nevertheless, this city was also a state — that is, it made its own laws, coined its own money, went to war or made peace with its neighbours entirely according to the wishes of its citizens. In a way, it was like a scale model of one of the giant states of today — a working model in which all the parts, though tiny, are in place. Scale models are always fascinating and this is one of the reasons why the story of Florence has been of such great interest for hundreds of years.

But Florence was more than a city or a state — much more. Between the years 1450 and 1500 —

the period of time with which this book is concerned — there were many other city-states, some of them bigger, richer and much more powerful than Florence. The real reason why Florence has made such a mark in history is because its citizens put into practice a very old idea and made it work so well that, even today, it affects almost everybody on earth. They called the idea 'Liberty' and they believed that each person had the right to do what he thought best for himself — so long as it did not hurt other people. The Florentines were certainly not saints: they could be as greedy and selfish and stupid as anybody else. But, every so often, they could stop what they were doing and ask themselves why they were doing it — and if the right thing to do was dangerous or unpleasant they had the courage and the good sense to go ahead and do it.

Looking back at Florence, even from this great distance of time, one can be almost bewildered by the sheer number of things that the Florentines produced. The city today is a priceless treasure-house of art. The great buildings themselves are some of the most beautiful ever erected and, inside them, are paintings and sculptures that are among the best ever produced by the hand of man. The museums of the world proudly display the tables and chairs, the goblets, plates, armour jewellery, made by Florentines for Florentines. The most treasured possessions of the great libraries of the word include the manuscripts lovingly created by Florentine scribes. But beautiful though these things are, and important though they are in the history of art, they are less important than the idea which produced them. 'Liberty' means different things to different people. For the Florentine, it meant the right — and the duty — to explore regions of the mind that other people had ignored. And, like real explorers, they brought back strange treasures with them.

1: TRAVELLER'S VIEW

The City stands in the centre of the State like a guardian and master. Towns surround her, just as the moon is surrounded by stars. The Florentine State might be compared to a round shield, with a series of rings surrounding a central knob. This central knob is the City itself, dominated by the *Palazzo Vecchio* (Old Palace) — a mighty castle, the centre of the whole shield. The rings around it are formed first by the walls and suburbs, then by a belt of country houses and estates, and finally by a distant circle of towns. Between the towns are cashes and towers reaching to the sky.

This was how a Florentine writer, Leonardo Bruni, described his city at the beginning of the fifteenth century, when it was at the height of its power, with many other cities and towns subject to it. His pride and love are obvious — his city is as beautiful as the moon and as strong as a shield. All Florentines shared that passionate love for their home. What Bruni does not say is that all the other towns in the state were held down by brute force. But this, after all, is what every other capital city was trying to do and probably Bruni thought it hardly worth mentioning.

A traveller approaching Florence at that time passed first through an undefended outer area, the 'belt of country houses and estates'. It is unlikely that the traveller would be journeying alone because, though there was little danger of bandits so close to the great city, the land permanently swarmed with soldiers. Most of them were mercenaries hired by the Florentine government to fight its enemies, but they were quite prepared to make up their pay by falling upon the weak and robbing them. There was not much the people could do about it, short of hiring more mercenaries to keep the first lot in check.

Imagine a traveller, then, in company with others of his kind — two or three merchants perhaps, a pilgrim or two, a government official returning home: all of them armed, and with an escort of their own hired soldiers. The road is unmetalled and dusty, but in excellent condition, for even at that time trade was Italy's lifeblood and the Florentines took a very large share of it.

The Italians have a particular word for the mixture of farmland, villages, and large houses that surround a city. They call it the *contado*, a word which cannot really be translated into English because the English have never developed anything quite like it and so do not need a descriptive word. The contado is to a city what a farm is to a castle: without it, the city would starve. The very first thing an invading enemy attempted was to destroy the crops and kill the peasants.

The peasants who tilled the lands of the contado had a very special relationship with the city. In time of war, they joined the citizens in their attack on the enemy. If the hostile army was too great, they turned to the city for refuge, together with their livestock and families. Unlike the wretched peasants in France, or even in England, at that time, they were no man's slaves. They farmed their own land or rented it from another man but in either case they were tough, fiercely independent people, as ready to pick up swords as spades.

After crossing this outer area of farmland, the traveller comes to a more park-like area dotted with villas. Every Florentine who could afford it had his villa in the country. Life in the narrow, crowded streets of the city was intolerable in the summer, with the heat trapped by the surrounding hills. Whether the villa was a huge mansion with hundreds of acres, or only a humble cottage with a wheat patch and a tiny vineyard, it was the place of escape to a calmer, healthier life. Here, in the cool of a summer evening, the Florentine was at home, away from the endless, jostling crowds. He could forget the ever present fear of a sudden riot which would bring armed men out in hundreds and leave the streets littered with dead and dying. Many good Florentine stories have their setting in a villa, where friends met at leisure, dining in the vineyard, gossiping, or perhaps plotting.

Finally, coming to the brow of one of the surrounding hills, the traveller saw Florence itself spread before him. A traveller even now sees a similar view — a beautiful city of honey-coloured stone, with here and there patches of grey or warm red or gleaming white. It looks less like a collection of individual buildings than one single vast palace, for walls and roofs and spires all combine to make a whole, once held in by the circuit of the enormous city walls. Today, as in the fifteenth century, the most distinctive feature is still the great red-brown dome of the Cathedral, towering above the low roofs of the city. This is Florence's greatest pride, completed a little over fifty years before our traveller's journey and already one of the wonders of Europe. There is a great fortified tower of grey stone too, soaring high into the air: this is the tower of the Palazzo Vecchio — the 'Old Palace' — the town hall of Florence.

But our fifteenth-century traveller also saw dozens of other towers, few of which exist today. They were similar to the tower of the Palace — grim buildings designed for warfare. At the base of each was what amounted to a castle — the town house of some great Florentine family. Warfare within the city was as incessant as warfare outside, and each family wanted a bigger and stronger house with a higher tower than its neighbours. The Florentine government, alarmed at the increasing number of these towers — each of which could protect a rebellious group — tore down dozens. But many still remained to give the traveller fair warning of what life in the city was like.

Descending the hill, the traveller came to the great Porta Romana — the Roman Gate. This is one of eleven gates which pierce the massive walls of the city. Some, like the Porta Romana, are named after the city which lies at the other end of the road they guard. Others take their names from some local feature: the Gate of Justice is so called because it is there that criminals were executed.

In the past the city walls were Florence's most important piece of architecture. For centuries Italy existed in a state of warfare between cities, and without walls, Florence would have been a helpless prey for its enemies. At the beginning of the fifteenth century the walls had twice been extended as the city grew, and there were already plans for building yet another extension.

The Porta Romana, as with the other ten gates, was more than just a way in and out. It was a small castle in its own right, with a permanent garrison. It sheltered customs officials as well, for there was a tax on almost everything that entered the city. Our traveller was probably asked to declare his business in Florence and, if he looked at all a suspicious character, a report about him was probably in the hands of the authorities in a very short time.

But Florence was, above all else, a trading city and people by the score passed in and out of the Porta Romana daily. The law-abiding traveller had nothing to fear, and was allowed in without formalities. The road from the gate passes an enormous private palace before it comes at last to the Arno, the river upon which Florence is built and which now divides the city roughly in two.

All Italian cities that stand on rivers inherited the Roman genius for bridge-building. Florence is no exception and there are four splendid bridges over quite a short length. London, by contrast, had only one bridge in the fifteenth century, and on a much longer length of river.

The road from the Porta Romana led — as it still does today — to the Ponte Vecchio, the 'Old Bridge'. The Roman bridge that once crossed the river here was swept away in a great flood 150 years before and the present bridge was built in 1345. Although quite narrow, shops and houses line it on each side. Looking along it, it appears to the traveller like an ordinary street, and he has to go to the edge to see the river below. In summer, the Arno sinks to the merest trickle in the middle of its stony bed. But in winter and early spring, when the river is fed by the melting snows of the Apennines in which it rises, it becomes a full, brown, hurtling torrent quite capable of sweeping a bridge away. It provides another source of food for the city, for there is a small but flourishing fishing industry along its banks.

Crossing the Ponte Vecchio, the traveller steps into the heart of Florence. Immediately in front of him is a piazza or square, and dominating it the Palazzo Vecchio, whose soaring tower is visible from the distant hill. The official name of the palace is the Palazzo della Signoria — *Sigrioria* being the name given to the city's government, and the square is called Piazza della Signoria after it. Piazza and Palazzo together form the true heart of Florence. Here the business of government was carried out, partly in the square and partly in the palace, and only too often in those days to the accompaniment of bloodshed.

2: HOW THE GOVERNMENT WORKED

In most countries of the world today, a government consisting of a few hundred people will make the laws that affect the lives of millions of their fellow countrymen. In theory, everyone has a chance to be elected to that government but, in practice, very few people will ever have a direct say in the making of laws.

This is unavoidable because of the huge size of modern populations. In a country with a population of, say, 30 million adults, there would have to be many thousands of people in the government if every adult were to have a turn at governing. This would be obviously unworkable and so a system has grown up in which a majority of the people elect a handful to govern on their behalf.

This would have seemed a gross injustice to a Florentine in the fifteenth century. In the first place, he thought of 'politics' as something which affected him, personally, in every aspect of his life. The original meaning of the word 'politics' asks the question 'What is the best way for people to live together?' Human beings prefer to live in groups — but how shall the rights of each person in a group be protected, and how shall the duties of each be defined? To take an active part in politics, therefore, was not only a duty but an exciting intellectual game — and the Florentine, above all else, loved getting into the middle of things and arguing.

There was another reason, a very strong one, for trying to take a direct part in government — self-protection, particularly if one were wealthy. 'It goes badly in Florence for anyone who possesses wealth without a share in the government,' Lorenzo de' Medici said truly. Florentine politicians were no more dishonest than others of their time. The safety of their city was their first duty, but they would have considered themselves as simpletons if they did not take advantage of the opportunity to look after themselves and their friends.

Because he loved politics as a fascinating game, and because he saw that it affected him vitally, the Florentine insisted that every citizen should have his turn at governing the city. At first sight, this seems quite sensible for there were only about 80,000 people living in the city. Children, of course, were excluded from governing and no one would have dreamt of allowing women to take any part in politics. At the most, there were perhaps 20,000 people who could reasonably hope to take part in the governing of their city and be called citizens.

And that was where the trouble started, for of that 20,000 less than a quarter had full rights. For generation after generation there were endless battles in the city between the few with power and the many who were trying to obtain some for themselves. And even when that struggle was ended, more battles broke out to decide, not who should govern the city, but how it should be governed.

In Florence, as in all Italian cities, there were two main political parties called Guelf and Ghibelline. Roughly — very roughly — they corresponded to what is today called left and right wing parties. The Guelfs, on the whole, represented the mass of poorer men: on the whole, they favoured increased democracy. The

Ghibellines were the aristocratic party, determined to keep things as they were.

But party labels were little more than an excuse for fighting. As soon as the Guelfs had triumphed over their opponents they split into two sections and went on fighting each other. The city suffered terribly, not only from the constant bloodshed but from the fact that when one party triumphed, its defeated opponents were expelled from the city. The great poet Dante was one of the people who were exiled in this manner. Florence, he said bitterly, was like a sick person tossing and turning on a bed, never at rest, always trying to find ease. The exiles often joined up with Florentine enemies outside, so that the city not only lost its best people, but found them turned into enemies.

At last the more reasonable people in Florence realised that the city was destroying itself and managed to pass a law which gave power to the greatest number of people. The wealth of Florence was based on its trade and manufactures. It was therefore decided that all members of the recognised trade guilds should be eligible for government. Even a nobleman would have to join a guild if he wanted a chance to govern.

The actual method of choosing men for the government was fairly simple. The city was divided into four quarters, each of which elected two men who were known as Priors. Three more men were elected in each quarter and these, known as Good Men, acted as advisers to the Priors. And at the very head of the government was an official who bore the splendid title of Standard-bearer of Justice. When he was elected he received a great banner, with the city's device of a red lily on a white ground, which was carried in all civic processions.

There were many more special offices — for taxation, for war, for trade — but the Standard-bearer, the eight Priors and the twelve Good Men were the supreme government: the Signoria. The word means 'Lordship' and these men were treated exactly as though they were lords during their brief period of office. They received no pay, but they lived at the public expense — and lived very well indeed in one of the most prosperous cities in Europe. They ate off gold or silver plate, their food and wine was of the choicest, they were entertained by the foremost *artistes* of the day. Each had his servants and each, for a few weeks, could feel that he was a person of consequence before going back to his trade of cobbler or goldsmith, weaver or butcher.

But there lay the weakness of the system — the fact that no office could be held for more than six months or, in some cases, for as little as eight weeks. This was necessary to ensure that everyone had his turn, but it made it extraordinarily difficult to run the government at all. If a new policy was introduced, the men who introduced it would find themselves out of office before they had had even a chance to see if it worked. The policy might be continued by the next people — or it might not.

Every few weeks Florence was plunged into turmoil as citizens scrambled for office. Threats, bribery and plain dishonesty were freely used. Other Italians were astonished by the constant Florentine upheavals. But at least the system worked, after a fashion. There was more bribery but less bloodshed.

It might have gone on working for a long time if one vital group had not been left out of it. All members of trade guilds were now recognised citizens, but there was a very large number of men who had no trade at all. They were unskilled labourers for the most part, men who did not possess the ability, or had never had the chance, to learn a proper trade. And these men found that they were totally excluded from government and all that went with it. They rebelled — and almost destroyed their own city. Briefly organised into a huge, revengeful mass, they terrorised Florence — burning, looting, murdering. After a few days the city was completely at their mercy and anything could have happened with a mindless mob in control.

But what did happen was a wonderful example of the Florentine genius for government. The mob had spilled into the Piazza della Signoria and were howling around the great palace, demanding the surrender of the Signoria. A man called Michael Lando — who worked at a humble job in a wool factory — glanced down and saw that the great Standard of Justice was lying in the dust. Lando may have been a rebel but he was also a Florentine, and no Florentine could see the Standard so dishonoured. He picked it up. The mob saw the great banner waving above their heads and immediately hailed the man who held it as Standard-bearer of Justice. 'If I am Standard-bearer I am therefore Lord of Florence', Lando said, and ordered the mob to go home. Incredibly, they obeyed and order returned.

Lando, clad just as he was in dirty, ragged clothes, marched into the palace and announced that he represented the people. The terrified government accepted him and over the next few days Lando worked out a new system which allowed the despised labourers to have a share in the government. What is perhaps the most astonishing thing is that power did not go to the head of this humble workman. He had saved Florence, but when his time came he resigned his office willingly and became just a workman again.

But the new system only patched up the old one. And soon this, too, broke down and Florence was in a worse position than before. The richer guilds — the bankers and goldsmiths and cloth merchants — could say with some truth that only disaster resulted when power was given to all the people. The poorer guilds — the butchers and cobblers and bakers — found themselves edged to one side again. They fought back and murderous battles began all over again in the streets of Florence.

There seemed to be only one way out of the situation. Other Italian cities had found that government by the people just did not seem to work, and had ended by giving all power to one man whom they called the prince. It meant that all had to obey his orders, but it also meant that order was restored. Was this, perhaps, the only way in which Florence could be saved?

3: THE MEDICI FAMILY

The Medici began their career in quite ordinary circumstances. Originally, they may have been physicians — for the word 'medici' means 'doctors' and the balls on their coat of arms may have been intended as pills. But little was known about them until about the year 1400 when the head of the family founded a bank.

That was the beginning of the family fortune. European trade was beginning to grow, merchants needed money to buy goods in one place so that they could sell them in another, and the Medici gained a reputation for honest dealing. They expected a lot back for their money — as much as 30 per cent — but they were prepared to lend not only to the wealthy and powerful but to anyone who, in their judgment, was likely to make a success. On one occasion they lent money to a poor young monk who apparently little chance of ever repaying it. Later he became the Pope and made the Medici his bankers.

Soon they had branches throughout Europe — in England, Germany, France — as well as in other Italian cities. They made a lot of money, but they gained something just as valuable, a knowledge of the world. In order to make good business decisions, they needed to know what was happening, which king was strong and which was weak, which man kept his word and which man did not. Their agents in the branches of the bank regularly sent them reports on local conditions. As a result, the Medici family knew more about what was happening outside, as well as inside, Florence than did the Florentine government itself.

Giovanni, the founder of the bank, took little part in politics, for he was content to be a businessman alone. His son, Cosimo, thought differently and when his father died, leaving him an enormous fortune, he decided to use part of it for the benefit of Florence.

Cosimo was forty years old when he became head of the family. He was well educated and had travelled widely. The richest man in Florence, he could have commanded what luxuries he wished: instead, he lived a simple life. He still continued the family business of banking, piling up even more money than did his father. But he also ran the farm on his villa as though he were an ordinary peasant, digging and planting and weeding with his own hands. Like so many Florentines, he was a great admirer of ancient Rome. In his private life he tried to copy the Roman virtues of simplicity, and in his public life he tried to lead Florence towards the more balanced, more peaceful system that he believed the Romans had enjoyed.

It was easy enough for him to get into the government with the powerful backing of his family. But it was also easy for him to arouse bitter jealousy. There were many other wealthy families in Florence, and they were growing alarmed at the increasing wealth of the Medici. They looked for an excuse to cut Cosimo down before he grew too big.

The excuse was quickly found. Florence had recently been defeated in one of its many wars with neighbouring cities and Cosimo was accused of supplying the enemy with money. It may have been true — he was, after all, a banker with money in almost every city in Italy — but he denied the charge and produced his accounts to show that he had given large sums to Florence to pay its soldiers. Nevertheless, he was convicted, and would probably have been condemned to death if he had not skilfully bribed some officials.

Instead of death, he was condemned to a punishment which most Florentines regarded as almost as bad — exile. Cosimo took the news calmly, as he took all news, good or bad. In any case he was in a far better position to lead a comfortable life in exile than most Florentines, because he could draw money from Medici banks almost anywhere. He went to Venice, where he was received like a prince, and settled down happily enough to spend his ten years' exile.

But Florence was not so happy. With the departure of Cosimo, the city lost the huge funds of the Medici bank. Everyone suffered — the little shopkeeper who wanted a small loan to tide him over a bad period, the wealthy man who wanted to borrow thousands for his daughter's dowry, and the State itself, which always needed money.

Exactly a year after he had left, the Florentines begged Cosimo to return. Graciously, he agreed to come back and as soon as he was installed in the fine new palace he had built in the city, he set about destroying his enemies. He did not do it in the old-fashioned way of murder, but in the better modern way of 'persuasion'. He let it be known that such and such a man met with his disapproval and sooner or later, that man would find himself condemned to exile, or forbidden to take part in the government.

With his powerful friends, Cosimo set about re-fashioning the machinery of government. Instead of turning the city upside-down every few weeks in order to elect a Signoria, a small permanent committee would choose the new government, drawing names out of a ballot box at regular intervals. Cosimo did not himself choose the members of that powerful committee — but somehow, only his friends were appointed to it.

Much of Cosimo's power sprang from the fact that very many men owed him money, or wanted to borrow money from him. Even so, the system could not have worked unless the Florentines wanted it to work. For the first time in many years, some sort of order came back to the city, and they welcomed it.

Power left Cosimo unchanged. If he had so wished it he could have become the Prince of Florence, answerable to no man but himself. But that, to his mind, would have been a wicked action and he continued as a simple citizen. As a result of his own experiment the taxes which the Medici bank had to pay soared high — but he went on paying them. At the same time he poured money into creating beautiful new buildings for the city, spending over four million pounds in modern money in the process. One of his gifts was the cloister of the convent of San Marco which you see in the picture on the next page.

Cosimo died at the ripe old age of seventy-four. He met death as calmly as he met everything else, preparing for it, as he said, as though he were going on a journey to another country.

Immediately after his death the Florentines begged his son to take over the government. They had known thirty years of peace under the Medici and believed that at last they had found the right system. Cosimo's son, Piero, ruled well, but he was in bad health and died after only five years.

Again, the Florentines begged the Medici to continue ruling the city. This time, the head of the family, Lorenzo was only twenty years old. He was extremely reluctant to take over the difficult task and pointed out that he was far too young. But the Florentines insisted and, at last, Lorenzo gave way.

Lorenzo de' Medici ruled Florence unofficially for twenty-three years and when he died, at the early age of forty-three, friends and enemies alike of Florence mourned his passing. The King of Naples spoke for all of them when he said: 'This man lived long enough for his own glory, but died too soon for Italy.'

Lorenzo was an ugly man — heavy featured with a remarkably large nose — but the charm of his personality was such that people completely forgot his physical appearance and spoke of him as an attractive man. He was an astonishing mixture of talents and moods. Today he would be drinking with rowdy companions in rough taverns: tomorrow, he would be engaged in deep philosophic argument with brilliant scholars. Like his father and grandfather he collected rare and beautiful books and had a splendid library built for them by Michelangelo. He wrote first-class poetry — but was also a very keen businessman with a wide grasp of commercial problems. He loved brilliant displays and festivals, but was also deeply religious, without losing tolerance for people of other religions. When a wandering preacher tried to stir up trouble against the Jews of Florence, Lorenzo had him quietly shown out of the city. And in addition to all these personal qualities, he was a supremely competent statesman, skilfully protecting Florence from its many enemies not by waging war but by negotiating, and building up alliances.

The grateful Florentines had given the title of 'Pater Patriae' — Father of his Country — to Lorenzo's grandfather, Cosimo. To Lorenzo himself they gave the title of 'Magnificent' and ever since he has been known simply as 'Lorenzo the Magnificent'. There is little wonder that, after the rule of two such men, the Florentines were convinced that their security and happiness were best left in the hands of a Medici. In the long run it proved a tragic decision, for none of the later Medici measured up to the standard set by Cosimo and Lorenzo, but during their long rule totalling nearly sixty years, Florence achieved the peak of its brilliant career.

4: THE GUILDS OF FLORENCE

A Florentine ambassador was sent to see the Duke of a neighbouring state who had been threatening to make war on Florence. In order to impress the ambassador with his wealth and power, the Duke took him into his treasury where great piles of glittering golden coins were displayed. Politely, the Florentine admired them and then picked up a handful. 'I see that these are all florins,' he said, 'for they are stamped with the Lily of Florence. If you have so many, how much more must we have — who make them.'

The Florentines were fond of this story because it was true. There had been a time when every city made its own coins, just as every country does today. But gradually, merchants found that the gold florin of Florence was accepted everywhere, for people knew that it was made of honest metal. Soon the florin was used all over Europe.

The tiny gold coin told two things about Florence. Its traders were honest, and they were wealthy. The gold which was made into coins came from many distant places. It might have come in the form of gold dust or golden bars or even as foreign coins. From Russia to Egypt, from London to Athens poured a steady stream of gold to buy the things that Florence produced. Other cities and countries grew wealthy through war. It was the Florentine boast that their wealth was made honestly, through trade and manufacture.

The workers of Florence had organised themselves into a number of guilds which they called Arts. In some ways, the Arts were like modern trade unions for they were originally formed by the workers themselves for their own protection. But while a trade union consists of the employees and is mostly concerned with working conditions, the Arts contained masters and workers. They were almost independent communities within the city, making their own laws and regulating almost every part of their members' lives.

The only possible way to enter an Art was to be nominated by one of the members. The usual thing was for a father to nominate his son. The boy would spend a long apprenticeship in the trade — two or three years, perhaps, if he wanted to be a baker, ten years or even more if he wanted to be a goldsmith. During his apprenticeship he would receive no money at all. His master would give him board and lodgings and treat him as one of the family — including such things as whipping him for disobedience and making sure that he went to church.

At the end of his apprenticeship, the young man would very carefully make one special piece of work. This was his 'masterpiece' — the piece of work which would decide whether or not he was fit to be a master craftsman. Guild officials would solemnly inspect the work and, if they approved it, he was free to work on his own and engage other craftsmen to work for him. Many men, however, found that they could not raise sufficient capital to start their own business and so they remained employees — but still had all their rights in the guild.

There were a few large factories in Florence, but most of the work was carried out by small groups consisting of a master, two or three craftsmen at most and perhaps a couple of apprentices. This was one of the reasons which originally made Florence a true democracy. A master and his craftsmen had passed through exactly the same apprenticeship, they worked side by side at the same bench, prayed together at their guild church, even fought together behind the guild banner. It was only when some of the guilds became very wealthy that a gap began to develop between master and man.

One of the reasons for the high standard of Florentine workmanship was the strict control which the officers of the guild exercised over their members. They had the right to inspect work at any stage, and to order the destruction of anything that did not come up to standard. The most minute regulations were laid down concerning quality of materials to be used, and any man who regularly broke the rules would find himself expelled from the guild, with no hope of finding employment in another.

By the time of the Medici there were fourteen main guilds in Florence, one for each recognised trade. The guild councils very closely resembled the Florentine government itself, with officials elected at regular intervals, to the accompaniment of great ceremony. The councils, indeed, actually formed part of the government, with the natural result that the leaders of the wealthy guilds almost controlled the city. The Medici, being the most important people in the very important guild of bankers, turned this fact to good account.

All members in a guild were equal — but the guilds themselves were far from equal. At one extreme, they were composed of such people as fishmongers, cobblers, or butchers: a master in these guilds was usually just an ordinary workman or shopkeeper, earning his living as best he could. The Florentines, with their love of nicknames, called the members of these poorer guilds the 'Thin People' while those in the wealthy trades were called 'Fat People'. Nearly all the troubles in Florence stemmed from the struggle between 'Thin' and 'Fat'.

The most powerful guilds in Florence were not the goldsmiths and bankers but those concerned with the manufacture of fabric for clothes. Comparatively few people could afford beautiful ornaments of gold, or had enough spare money to lend it to banks. But everyone needed clothes

— in Europe generally as well as Florence. Florentine traders soon recognised the value of this ordinary but important trade, and eventually one man in three in Florence was working in the wool, silk, or cloth industry.

Originally, rough cloth was imported into the city and there the skilled hands of Florentine craftsmen turned it into a beautiful, finished product, dyed in wonderful colours and ornamented with elaborate patterns in brocade. The finished cloth would continue on its travels across half the world, earning more gold for Florence.

This trade continued, but at the same time there began to develop the woollen trade which did all the processes of clothmaking from fleece to the finished product. Most of the wool came from England — by the fifteenth century Florence was England's biggest single customer. The wool arrived in great bales, in the same condition that it left the sheep's back. It was necessary to clean it, card it and generally prepare it for the weaving stage. Hundreds of unskilled workmen were brought in for this tedious, unpleasant job. They were not considered fit to be true craftsmen and therefore formed that large underprivileged group who had no rights in the city.

But the other workmen enjoyed good pay and conditions for their work was highly skilled. One of the most important of the wool corporations was that of the dyers. Sober browns, blues and black were not popular. People wanted colour, and they got it: yellow and scarlet, red, pink, blue, crimson. Dyeing was a highly skilled craft for the colours came from natural materials whose value could easily be destroyed through clumsy handling. Crocuses in spring provided the brilliant yellow. Vermilion was obtained from lichen, madder was obtained by crushing the bodies of certain insects. Materials for other colours were transported over great distances from the East, or were family secrets that sometimes died with the last member of the family.

Every year Florence produced over 70,000 pieces of cloth. Each piece was carefully examined by the guild officials and, if passed, was stamped with the seal of the guild. A tag was fixed to it, detailing exactly how much it had cost at various stages of its manufacture, including the many taxes that had been paid out during its journey from the back of an English sheep to its arrival in a shop. The person who bought a piece from that roll of cloth, whether he was in Germany or Egypt, England or Greece knew that his purchase was guaranteed by a powerful Italian organisation most jealous for its international good name.

5: THE FLORENTINE AT HOME

The impression of Florence given by the scores of Florentines who wrote about their city is one of solid comfort. In many other cities of Italy, particularly in Naples and Rome, there was a great gap between the very rich and very poor. Splendid palaces furnished with priceless articles shared the same street with broken down hovels, swarming beggars rubbed shoulders with arrogant nobles dressed in gorgeous costume.

The Florentine disliked excess in anything, believing that too much wealth was as bad as too little. One of the reasons why the Medici were once expelled from the city was because they had built themselves a palace too princely for an honest citizen. There was a saying, rather similar to the English phrase 'too big for his boots', which was applied to anyone who seemed to be getting above himself. If he did not take warning he was likely to find himself the centre of unwelcome attention from a hostile crowd. Most Florentines, therefore, contrived to live comfortably, but soberly. A man should be as generous and as hospitable as possible, but he must not show off.

The first thing a visitor from the north would notice was the cleanliness of the streets and the solidity of the houses. Even in London at that time, most of the streets were unpaved, so that they became muddy gullies in winter, and the great majority of houses were made of wood. In Florence, on the other hand, even a humble citizen could hope to have a two-storey house made of stone, facing on to a neatly paved street which was regularly cleaned. He counted cleanliness very high indeed. If his house was too small to have the huge tub that was used as a bath, he and his family could use one of the public baths provided at the expense of the city.

A merchant or shopkeeper would have his office or shop on the ground floor. Windows were rather small and all of them had good, stout shutters for one never knew when a riot would start in the street outside. Inside, the houses were somewhat dark and could be very cold in winter, for most floors were made of brick or stone. Most of the bigger houses had fireplaces, and even real chimneys, but in the smaller ones the family made do with a brazier. In very cold weather people hugged little earthenware jars filled with red-hot coals. The day began very early — soon after daybreak — and so most people were in bed not long after sunset. But if they wanted light, they used the same sort of light that the Romans had used and which is still used in country districts in Italy — lamps supplied with olive oil. Wax candles were used only by the very rich and in churches.

There were not many rooms in the house by modern standards. Some very large houses had as many as fourteen rooms, with two or perhaps three rooms set apart for the use of guests, and sometimes two kitchens, one on each floor. But this was only for very wealthy owners. Most people had a single, large room downstairs for cooking, eating and general purposes and upstairs the floor area would be partitioned into rooms as they were required. Nobody troubled much about privacy and bedrooms would lead one into the other. Well-to-do families had servants and even slaves, but there were no servants' quarters. Each servant was provided with a folding bed but had to find a place to put it every night — in the kitchen, perhaps or, if she were very favoured, she might share one of the family bedrooms. This rather makeshift system was adopted for other purposes. The bath-tub — a round, wooden tub — was brought into the bedroom; and the lady of the house used the main bedroom as a kind of reception room.

One of the attractive things in many houses was a kind of open court called the *loggia*. Usually it was built on to the side of the house; less often it was built on top and so formed the upper floor. The roof was held up by pillars round which grapevines were trained, the beautiful plant being both decorative and useful. Here in the loggia, in summer, friends of the family were entertained to meals.

Most families had only two main meals in the day. The head of the house might perhaps snatch a cup of wine and a morsel of bread on rising, but the first meal was not until 10 a.m. Fruit, bread, watered wine and perhaps some sort of sausage were eaten at breakfast. Supper was taken before darkness fell. This was a more elaborate meal. The traditional Italian dish of pasta —

dough made into various shapes such as macaroni or ravioli — formed the main dish, for most people could afford meat only about once a week. But there would be plenty of salad, cheese and fruit, and sweet cakes and jellies to finish the meal. Wine was always served, even to children. Few houses had their private water supply from a well, and water was always rather suspect for one could never be sure it was pure. But even the poorer Florentines had their own little vineyards and the wine they made, though rather harsh to the taste, was considered to be a far healthier drink than water from public wells.

People spent their money on food and clothes. Furniture was considered relatively unimportant so that the house of even a wealthy man would seem curiously bare to modern eyes. Poorer people still used rushes on the floor, but most had woven mats and even, perhaps, a small carpet which was prized as a family heirloom. The walls were distempered: here and there a local painter might attempt a simple design or two to enliven the blank walls. Really wealthy men like the Medici would commission an artist to decorate the room with, perhaps, a mythological scene, or a scene from the Bible, or even portraits of the family.

The main hall was furnished with a dining table, a chair for the master of the house and perhaps another for his wife, and benches for everyone else. The bedroom was even more bare — but what it lacked in furnishing was made up by the splendour of the bed. This was the most important item of furniture. Usually it was so big that it would not go through the door in one piece and so had to be put together in the room. It was furnished with a canopy and curtains which could be drawn and so make a little private room — one of the few places were there was any privacy in the house. In Florence, where so many people worked in the cloth trade, the bed linen was quite good, but mattresses were stuffed with straw.

In every house, rich or poor, there would be one specially cherished piece of furniture in the bedroom in addition to the bed. This would be the 'cassone', a large wooden chest for linen which every girl received on marriage. Even the daughter of poor parents would expect to receive her cassone, plain and roughly finished though it might be. The daughter of wealthy people would receive a work of art. In some parts of Italy the fashion was to carve the chest with beautiful figures and designs, but the Florentines usually preferred to have them painted and some of the foremost artists of the day would be engaged to produce this piece of furniture that marked a girl's passing from girlhood to marriage.

In all families at all times it is the woman who runs the home. A Florentine woman was fortunate in that she was accepted on almost equal terms with men. She had no say in running the city, her property became her husband's (for he was her legal master), and no decent woman would go to places of public entertainment. But in her home she entertained her husband's guests and was accepted into their conversation.

Few people bothered about a girl's education — as far as book-learning was concerned. The old-fashioned, indeed, thought that books could only corrupt a girl. But what she did learn at her mother's side was vital. Most of the things that a family required were produced in the house itself. In autumn a good housewife had to make sure that sufficient food was preserved for the long months of winter ahead and many busy days were spent at the skilled work of pickling meat, drying vegetables and preserving fruit. Clothes had to be made all the year round, as well as repaired — some women even wove the cloth itself.

A housewife had to know something about medicine. There were plenty of doctors in the city, but their fees were high and, in any case, their hit-or-miss methods did not make people trust them much. A girl would learn from her mother — who had learnt it from her mother — what herbs would cure what diseases, where they could be found and how prepared. There was much to occupy a girl's time at home, and in an interesting way. She was probably glad, not envious, that she could not accompany her brother to the schoolmaster's house where he learned Latin grammar, a little history and mathematics. Florentine education was better than in many other places; the children, at least, were beaten less often. But for ordinary people it was still very narrow and extremely dull.

A girl who was not married before she was twenty began to worry if she would ever be married at all. Sixteen was the usual age for a girl to be married and the better-off her parents were, the less choice she had in the matter of a husband. The marriage would usually be arranged by a professional matchmaker, between people in the same class of society. The most important item was the dowry — that is, the money which the bride brought to her husband. A merchant in a fair way of business would be expected to provide a dowry of about 3,000 florins — roughly £9000 in modern English currency, and even a poor workman would have to find the equivalent of three or four years' pay to bestow on his daughter. A prudent man would start saving as soon as his daughter was born. The only alternative was to borrow the money at a heavy rate of interest, and remain in debt for many years to come. If a father declined to find the money, his daughter remained unmarried, or found a totally unsuitable husband. It was a hard custom, but it did ensure that a young couple set up home with some financial backing — a very important point when there were no social services to help them over the accidents of sickness or unemployment. Charitable people sometimes left money to provide a public dowry fund, and the State, too, might 'dower' a penniless girl.

After the contract had been signed, and the dowry paid over, the wedding took place. And here the Florentines threw their customary sobriety to the winds. So much money was spent on weddings, indeed, that the State even laid down regulations which were supposed to curb the expense. The regulations prescribed how much was to be spent on the banquet, even laying down how many courses there were supposed to be. Gifts to guests were forbidden and the entertainment was limited to a total of two days.

The regulations were largely ignored — to enforce them the Signoria would have been obliged to arrest every wedding party. When Lorenzo de' Medici married the daughter of a Roman prince in June 1469 more than a thousand guests were entertained in the Medici palace. Five banquets were served over a period of three days: 150 calves and 4,000 chickens were provided as well as an endless flow of expensive wine. The streets leading to the palace were decorated with garlands and ribbons, and mounted musicians preceded the bride. The ordinary people enjoyed it immensely for although only notables attended the banquet, the food leftover was by custom distributed among the crowds. A vast quantity of cheaper wine was also provided for them, as well as the splendid public entertainments which they had come to expect from the Medici.

Lorenzo's marriage was, of course, arranged for him. His mother went specially to Rome to look the bride over and decided that, although she was rather shy and uncultured, she would make a good wife for her son — as well as bring a handsome dowry to the Medici.

Lorenzo was very attached to his mother. In her day, she had been one of the beauties of Florence but she possessed brains as well as good looks and young Lorenzo was brought up in a home where books and music and art were considered as important as money and politics. His education began when he was five years old and he was soon doing Greek and Latin. He learnt to sing and play on the lyre and write verses.

Much of his boyhood was spent in the beautiful Medici villa. It was there that he gained his love of nature, which went side by side with his love of art. Here he went hunting and hawking with his tutor and other members of the family. In Florence he lived in the new Medici palace, a building which, to our eyes, looks more like a prison than a private house. But times were still unsettled in Florence and a private house could be called upon to serve as a fort at a moment's notice.

Lorenzo's married life was not particularly happy. His wife, Clarice, had a rather solemn view of life and though Lorenzo was as sincerely religious as she was, she was shocked by his love of gaiety and the fact that he seemed able to make friends of the most unlikely and unsuitable people. Lorenzo's strongest friend and ally was his brother, Giuliano, a handsome young man four years younger than himself who was extremely popular with the Florentine people. The greatest personal tragedy in Lorenzo's life was when Giuliano was murdered in a plot that nearly succeeded in killing Lorenzo himself. Lorenzo consoled himself a little by adopting

Giuliano's orphan son — who later became a pope.

Lorenzo had three sons of his own. We can tell that they got on well with their father from some letters which Piero, the eldest, wrote to Lorenzo when the family was sent away from Florence for a while for safety. In one he says that he and his sister, Lucrezia, are having a competition to see who can write best. If he wins, Piero says, can he have a pony? Whether he won or not, he got the pony which he describes when thanking his father for it as 'so handsome and so perfect'. In another letter he tells his father about all the family:

> We are all well and studying. Giovanni is able to spell. You can see for yourself how my writing is getting on. As for Greek, I work at it with Martin's help [Martin was his tutor], but do not get very far. Giuliano can only laugh. Lucrezia sews, sings and reads. Maddalena knocks her head against the wall but does not hurt herself. Luigia can talk quite a lot. Contessina makes a great noise all over the house. Nothing is wanting to use but to have you here.

Lucrezia also wrote letters asking for things — to her grandmother this time. She asked for a 'basket of roses which you promised me', for a fine embroidered sash, and for sugarplums to give to her younger brothers and sisters.

Lorenzo used to say about his three sons that one of them was good, one was wise and one was a fool. Unfortunately for the family it was the 'fool', Piero, who succeeded him as lord of Florence and so earned the dislike of the Florentines as nearly to destroy the Medici power in Florence. It was, perhaps, not altogether his fault. He liked hunting better than books, and though, as a boy, he tried to please his father by studying, he does not seem to have had many brains. Among Lorenzo's daughters, Lucrezia was the clever one.

6: THE ARTISTS OF FLORENCE

One of the reasons why it is possible to go back in time and obtain a vivid picture of a long-vanished society is because of the work of the most famous group of Florentines — the artists. In picture galleries throughout Europe, as well as in Florence itself, there are treasured the paintings which show us the world that the artists knew.

But painting was only one of the arts in which the Florentines excelled. They were also masters of the two great sister arts of architecture and sculpture. Scattered throughout the city today are superb buildings which have remained largely unchanged from the day they were built. The particular building may be a church or a private house, a palace, a government office — or even a prison — but they all have one thing in common. Each was recognised as a work of art as soon as it was completed and succeeding generations of Florentines have cherished it so that today, 500 years afterwards, a visitor can enter and see almost exactly what citizens of that distant period saw.

Most of the buildings and paintings that make Florence a living treasure-house were produced in an astonishing burst of activity over a very short period — roughly from about 1420 to 1520. The most famous part of this period was round about the 1480s when Lorenzo de' Medici was leading Florence.

This period of time is called the Renaissance. The word literally means 're-birth', and to a certain extent that was what happened — the ancient world of classical Greece and Rome was 'reborn' in Italy.

Scholars began it all. Working in dusty, forgotten libraries, they took part in one of the most exciting detective stories of history, tracking down the books and letters that had been written in the days of ancient Rome. After the fall of the Roman Empire these priceless works of learning had been scattered and lost. People had been far too busy keeping alive to worry about the fact that education had almost come to an end. Much that the Greeks and Romans had discovered about the world — in science, art and philosophy — was forgotten.

The discovery of the lost works was like opening a window in a darkened room. It brought in light, and at the same time opened a view into a much wider world. At the beginning there was a fashion, amounting to a craze, for anything Roman. Scholars refused to write in any language but Latin and the only true art was believed to be that which most closely resembled Roman or Greek art. The young sculptor Michelangelo found that it was easier to sell a statue that looked like Roman work than it was to sell his own, genuine work. The man who bought it from him pretended that it had been dug up and sold it, at a great profit, as a Roman discovery.

Before the fifteenth century the artist was treated just like any other craftsman — and a rather humble one at that. If he were a sculptor or an architect, he had to join the guild of Masons. No one quite knew where to put a painter, but because he had to join a guild, he was enrolled among the doctors and apothecaries — probably because he had to know a little chemistry to prepare his colours. Artists remained completely unknown by name. When a church was being built a mason might carve the most exquisite figures, but no more dreamed of putting his name on them than another mason dreamed of putting his name on the ordinary block of stone he had squared up. The painter, too, might turn from painting doors and windows and create a perfect work of art on a wall — but it was just a decoration and he would be laughed at if he tried to claim it as his own.

In addition to the strict control which his guild exerted on an artist was the even stricter control which the Church exerted on the work he created. Until about 1400 the Church was the biggest patron of artists and the art produced for it was naturally religious. The artist was strictly forbidden to invent new ways to re-tell the ancient story of Christianity. He had to follow the traditional ways, even down to using the same colour for costumes — the Madonna, for instance, was always shown in blue.

One of the first of the great Florentine artists to break away from the rigid controls of guild and Church was a man called Filippo Brunelleschi.

His father had wanted him to be a doctor but, instead, he became a goldsmith. Later he, too, became enthusiastic about Roman remains.

Instead of studying ancient Rome in the quietness of libraries as other people did, Brunelleschi went to the best place of all to do so — Rome itself. In his day, the great city was in a sad state. Most of the temples and palaces had long since been destroyed and squalid hovels were built on their site. But, patiently, he examined the ruins, and after twelve years he was convinced that now he understood how the Romans had been able to create their gigantic buildings.

It happened that, at this time, work on the great cathedral in Florence had come to a standstill. The main structure had long since been completed, but the architect had died and no one knew how to build a dome large enough to cover the enormous space left for it. The problem was how to support the dome while it was being built and the Wool Guild, who had been given the responsibility of building the cathedral, called a meeting to discuss the matter. Someone suggested that a huge mound of earth should be heaped up in the church and the dome built on top of it.

Brunelleschi laughed at the idea, and said he could do the job without using support at all. They thought he was mad, but so confident was he that he could copy the methods of the Romans, that at last the Wool Guild gave him the job. Work began in August 1420. Twelve years later the dome was half finished, everything was going smoothly, when suddenly Brunelleschi was sent to prison. The members of the Masons' Guild were furious that a non-mason should have been given such an important task. They used successfully the Florentine law that non-members of a guild should not engage in work performed by that guild and Brunelleschi was convicted.

But the Wool Guild was even more furious when they saw how work stopped abruptly — and they were far richer and more powerful than the Masons. Brunelleschi was pardoned, his accusers themselves sent to prison, and work continued on the dome, to be finished triumphantly sixteen years after it had started.

The new cathedral towered over a smaller black and white building that had been the cathedral of

Florence for longer than any man could remember. It was called the Baptistery, and was so old that Florentines believed that it had been built by Romans at the time of Julius Caesar. In it there had been a baptismal font so large that a person could be completely immersed in the holy water. Dante, the poet, once saved a young boy from drowning in it. The Florentines never lost their love for the ancient Baptistery, even after they had acquired a splendid new cathedral. While Brunelleschi was labouring on the giant dome of the cathedral another artist, Lorenzo Ghiberti, was making two superb bronze gates for the Baptistery. The work took him the better part of forty years and when it was finished a proud Florentine said: 'It is the most beautiful work of the world that was ever seen among ancients or moderns.' Even the great Michelangelo said: 'They are so beautiful that they would do well for the Gates of Paradise.'

Not far from the Baptistery rose a beautiful tower of coloured marble — the *campanile* or bell tower of the cathedral. It is usually called 'Giotto's tower' after the great artist who designed it, but he died before it was completed and two more architects succeeded him, one after the other, over the next fifty years before the work was brought to a conclusion. The Cathedral, the Baptistery and the Tower were quite different from each other, but in an almost magical way they seemed to combine and so make a kind of second heart for Florence — the religious heart to balance the political heart formed by the Palazzo Vecchio and its great square.

Florentine artists used many different kinds of material to decorate their city — not only marble of different colours, woodcarving and bronze, but pottery as well. A family named Della Robbia discovered how to make sculptures in terracotta, which they painted and glazed. You can still see pictures like the one below decorating the outside walls of buildings in Florence. Along the outside wall of the home for foundling children there are small round pictures of babies tightly bound up in the swaddling clothes which mothers used then.

Brunelleschi's battle with the Masons won an important victory for the artists — that they did not have to be members of guild to produce and sell their work. It was the beginning of the period when artists would be known by name, and their individual works become the prized possessions of the great ones of the land.

An artist still had to serve an apprenticeship, but it was more informal than under the guild system. A lad who felt that he wanted to paint looked for employment in the workshop of an established painter. At first his tasks were humble enough — cleaning up, grinding and preparing colours. Only gradually was he allowed to take part in real painting.

The fashion of the day favoured very large pictures — usually painted on walls, when they were called murals — which were crowded with detail. The master painter rarely did all the work himself. He planned the whole scheme, sketched in the main outlines and painted the important figures and faces. The rest of the work was done by apprentices. It was very highly skilled work. The Florentines adopted a process of wall painting called fresco. Plaster was laid on the wall and, while it was still wet, the picture would be painted upon it. Plaster dries very rapidly so not only did the painter have to work very fast, but only small sections could be done at a time. The artist could have no second thoughts. If he made a mistake the whole section had to be cut out and replastered.

Although many hands were at work on one painting, the finished picture had to look as though it had been done by one man and an apprentice became very skilful at copying his master's style. In many pictures, indeed, it is now impossible to say for certain which sections were done by the master and which by his pupils.

The Florentines still favoured religious subjects in paintings. The convent of San Marco, which Cosimo often visited, was full of paintings by Fra Angelico, who loved doing joyful angels in gold and red and blue. He painted a picture in each friar's cell which you can still see. Here is the *Annunciation* he painted at the top of the stairs. But mythology and Greek and Roman history were becoming very popular. The thing which strikes the modern observer of these pictures is that the artists did not care about what we now call historical accuracy. Whether the artist was painting a scene from the Bible, from Roman history or Greek mythology he clothed all his figures in what was, for him, modern dress. Jesus Christ was painted dressed like a Florentine scholar, Apollo like any young dandy seen in the streets. Julius Caesar was given the weapons of a Florentine soldier. Even the backgrounds were Florentine, so that Jerusalem was pictured to look almost exactly like Florence, and the Greek countryside was, in effect, drawn from the countryside that the artist knew personally.

Perhaps the most famous example of this kind of painting is the beautiful mural which Benozzo Gozzoli painted for the Medici palace. He took as his subject the journey of the Magi. In earlier representations of this story, the Magi are shown travelling alone or, at most, with one or two servants. Gozzoli created an enormous procession for them, every member of which is dressed in the height of Florentine fashion. In addition, he included realistic portraits of the Medici family in the procession as it wound its brilliant way through a fanciful landscape. In the front is Lorenzo as a young boy, seated on a beautiful white horse. Behind him, on another white horse, is his father Piero and beside Piero is old Cosimo, dressed in sober blue. The painter has even included himself — he is the person in the group behind Cosimo with his name painted in gold on his hat.

It had long been the fashion for the artist to insert the portrait of his patron in religious pictures — the patron is usually shown adoring the central subject. But now it was becoming more and more common for the artist to include his own portrait. Michelangelo did so in his terrible 'Last Judgment' in Rome and, more light-heartedly, Sandro Botticelli painted himself frankly looking at the spectator with a slightly quizzical expression. Botticelli painted another biblical subject which, in its way, is as perverse as Gozzoli's. 'Tobias and the Angel' is a Bible story, but shows Tobias as a handsome Florentine youth, and the Angel — though rather fancifully dressed — would probably attract little attention in Florence if his wings were removed; and the stern landscape of Palestine has given way to the gentle landscape of Tuscany. In his youth, Botticelli delighted in 'pagan' subjects and created paintings of classical myths that have a wonderful feeling of springtime freshness about them. *The Birth of Venus* tells the Greek story of how the goddess of love was wafted in a scallop shell from her birthplace in Cyprus to Greece, and the great painting known simply as *Primavera* (Springtime) shows the goddess Flora, attended by the graces, scattering the flowers of spring. The beautiful faces of the women in Botticelli's pictures have an expression of gentle sadness and it is not surprising to learn that, in later life, he seems to have turned completely towards religion. Many believe that he came under the influence of the great reformer Savonarola, and certainly the paintings of his later years were almost all of religious subjects. But they were far different from the stiff, formal pictures of earlier periods, for he carried into them the same fresh liveliness that made his mythological pictures a delight.

The Florentine artist was probably perfectly aware that an ancient Roman or Hebrew or Greek did not dress like a modern Florentine, but his intense pride in his own city and his own times made him indifferent to what would shock a twentieth-century painter. It is fortunate for us that he adopted this attitude because, looking at his picture of Jews in Jerusalem or Romans in

Rome we see Florentines in fifteenth-century Florence. For instance, behind the high altar in the Church of Santa Maria Novella you can see Florentine ladies in beautiful stiff dresses coming to greet a new-born baby, and a group of men with shrewd faces whom the Florentines would have recognised as well-known people.

When the apprentice painter felt that he had learned all he could from his master, he would try to set up on his own. And this was where the Renaissance painter was far more fortunate than those of earlier times. He could hope to find a private patron — a rich man who would provide him with the very expensive materials he needed and leave him to paint the picture in his own way.

The richest men in Florence were the Medici, and in generously using their wealth to encourage art they became probably the greatest art patrons of all time. Old Cosimo established the tradition, paying scores of thousands of florins to architects and painters and sculptors. Sculpture was his favourite art and it was for Cosimo that the young sculptor Donatello created his *David* the first truly Renaissance statue. Cosimo's son Piero continued the tradition — but painting was his choice and he was not above interfering and telling the artist what to do. The greatest patron even among the Medici was Lorenzo, excelling in this as he did in everything else. He was not content to wait until an artist had proved himself but went out of his way to find promising youngsters, providing them with food and shelter and pocket money until they were able to stand on their own feet.

It would be a foolish task to try to name the 'best' or the 'greatest' of the Florentine artists of this time. Each of them created something that no other person could have created. But even in this brilliant gathering there are two artists who, in very different ways, stand out from the crowd: Michelangelo and Cellini.

Michelangelo's father was a poor but proud country gentleman, and he strongly disapproved of the idea of his son becoming an artist. But Michelangelo had his way and was apprenticed to Ghirlandaio, the foremost artist of the day. The story is told that one day, during the absence of his master, Michelangelo made a drawing of the various tools they were using. 'He knows more than I do,' Ghirlandaio exclaimed when he saw the drawing and, very generously, drew Lorenzo de' Medici's attention to the brilliant apprentice.

Michelangelo was then thirteen years old, and for the next four years he lived as a member of Lorenzo's family — eating at the same table, studying under the same scholars as Lorenzo's own children. At the same time he worked hard in the art school that Lorenzo had established. He quarrelled with one of his fellow pupils — a bigger youth called Torrigiani — who claimed to be a better artist. Torrigiani settled the argument by dealing Michelangelo such a terrible blow on his face that his nose was broken — a disfigurement that Michelangelo bore for the rest of his life.

Michelangelo was eighteen years old when Lorenzo de' Medici died in 1492. Florence was plunged into chaos for Lorenzo's son Piero was extravagant and unpopular, and after two years the Florentines chased him out of the city. Michelangelo, because he had been a friend of the Medici, thought it safer to leave Florence at once. All his life he was to be affected unpleasantly by politics, even though he took no particular interest in them. He came back to

Florence a few months later and then took the road to Rome.

The great city was enjoying its own renaissance at that time for the Popes were determined to make it the most splendid city in the world. Michelangelo thought of himself first and foremost as a sculptor — he had an engaging habit of signing his letters 'Michelangelo, sculptor'. It was as a sculptor that he began a task that was to occupy him for nearly forty years — an immense tomb for Pope Julius II. The work was never finished — in Florence today can be seen some of the unfinished figures that were to adorn the tomb — figures that still bear chisel marks. Pope Julius changed his mind and forced Michelangelo to undertake a work that he hated, but which brought him even more fame. This was the decoration of the ceiling of an immense building called the Sistine Chapel with pictures showing the Creation of the world and other scenes. Even a visitor finds it difficult to look up at the ceiling for more than a few minutes at a time: Michelangelo worked at it for four years almost single-handed, lying flat on his back much of the time.

As though he were not content to produce some of the greatest painting and sculpture the world has ever seen, in his later years Michelangelo turned to poetry, architecture and even engineering. He did not have a happy life — his nature was far too stormy and suspicious for that. But he had a remarkably full and rich one and that, in the eyes of Florentines, was even more important.

Benvenuto Cellini was born in 1500 when Michelangelo was twenty-five years old. Cellini could not have been more different, both as artist and as man. Michelangelo wrought works which were immense both in size and idea: Cellini was a goldsmith excelling at tiny, beautiful figures. He created some wonderful statues — in particular one of Perseus slaying the Gorgon which today stands in an honoured position in the Piazza della Signoria. But perhaps his most famous work was a salt cellar. It was made as a table ornament and, though small, it is crowded with exquisite figures, any one of which would be a work of art in its own right.

Cellini was a gay, happy-go-lucky man who always seemed to come to the top. He was sent to prison for stealing the Pope's crown; he served as a gunner in one of the many Italian wars; he was continually quarrelling with fellow artists and employers — quarrels which were frequently settled with a sword. He murdered at least one man, and killed another who had murdered his brother. But he survived it all and in his old age wrote a delightful story of his own life. He was not very worried about telling the truth — particularly where he wanted to show himself as being clever or brave. But the book is so packed with vivid details, and written in such lively language that it has become world famous and is perhaps the best possible means of entering into the life of an artist of those brilliant and dangerous days.

7: HIGH DAYS AND HOLIDAYS

A crowd of Florentines with naked swords in their hands and the cry of 'Liberty' on their lips was perhaps the most terrifying sight any man could wish to encounter. But the same crowd of people, clad in their best clothes and bent on pleasure, was remarkably good-humoured and gay, prepared to share food and drink with total strangers, tolerant of the odd ways of foreigners, insatiably curious — altogether, a group of unusually attractive human beings.

It was still possible to tell what a man did by what he wore. Members of the learned professions wore the long gown that the Florentines called the *lucco*. A rare and beautiful shade of pink was reserved for the members of the Signoria, while doctors and lawyers dressed in dark purple. Old-fashioned people still preferred to wear this graceful garment but most younger people now wore a heavy, blouse-like upper garment and tights which combined the function of trousers and stockings.

Older people preferred darker colours and wore their hair at shoulder length. Young men cut their hair short, wearing it in a kind of bob which covered the forehead and ears, and wore a startling variety of colours. Some very rich young men wore velvet doublets in which gold thread and jewels were worked, and poorer youths would put themselves in debt to appear gorgeously dressed in the streets.

The Florentine government many times tried to put a curb on this wasteful personal expenditure. With the Florentine love for making laws, the government laid down the most minute regulations which said what a particular person in a particular walk of life could wear. Certain unfortunate officials prowled the streets, with instructions to question anybody who seemed to be breaking the law. It was an impossible task. As one of these officials said: 'If I ask a woman why she is wearing a forbidden headband, she tells me it is a garland. I stop another woman, saying "you mustn't wear buttons", and she tells me they are not buttons but toggles. I ask another why she is wearing ermine. It isn't ermine, says she. It's a suckling. And what, I ask, is a suckling? A kind of animal, she replies. It's no use!'

So the Florentines wore what they pleased. The old-fashioned were particularly shocked by the women's new styles — painted faces, dyed hair, elaborate dresses of silk and gold — and even versions of men's clothing. But it was impossible to change public opinion and fashion by law, as the Signoria had found when they tried to control wedding expenditure, and the new fashions grew ever more gaudy and expensive as Florence itself grew wealthier.

There were no long weekends and fixed holidays for the workers as we have nowadays: people worked from dawn till dusk usually for six days of the week. But over the year they enjoyed probably more free time than even a modern worker, for every saint's day was a holiday — and there were many saints' days in the calendar, each of which was celebrated with public as well as religious festivals.

The most popular was undoubtedly the Feast of St John the Baptist. He was the patron saint of Florence, whose head appeared on all the coins. Preparations were made weeks beforehand and on the day itself Florence appeared in a blaze of colour. Each guild strove to outdo the others by decorating its shops and the streets leading to them: the wealthy used gold cloth, the poorer anything that made a bright splash of colour.

The celebrations began with a religious service — as all celebrations began — but even this was like a theatrical display for in the processions leading to the Church of St John were people dressed as angels, saints, and characters from the Bible. Each guild would march behind its banners, forming an immensely long crocodile that wound its way endlessly through the city. Musicians and singers accompanied them, and there were probably as many people in the procession as there were watching.

In the evening a public entertainment in the Piazza della Signoria displayed work on which many people had laboured devotedly. Sometimes the entire square was turned into a kind of fairy castle in which a play from Florence's past was acted. The greatest artists did not disdain to contribute their skill, creating beautiful works intended to last only for the day — ships that seemed to sail across the square, trees full of exotic mechanical birds, wonderful giants that strode fearsomely through the crowd, monsters that breathed smoke and fire. Sometimes there was a tournament with the youths of one guild, or from one particular quarter of the city, pitted against another. They often ended in bloodshed but the Florentines were used to that and marshals were posted to stop the tournament if it looked like turning into a general riot.

Perhaps the most exciting event in Florentine eyes was the *palio*. This was a horse race through the streets of Florence itself. Rules were very flexible — indeed, they might as well have not had any rules at all. The riders had only one object — to get to the finishing post first. Everyone got off the streets, crowding into doorways, leaning out from windows, cheering wildly as the cavalcade thundered through the city from one side to the other. The winner received the palio, a piece of beautiful crimson cloth which he displayed proudly in his home.

That was the Feast of St John. But every guild had its own patron saint upon whose day the members would march in proud procession and there were in addition the other great feasts of the Church's year. The modern custom is to celebrate Christmas above all other Christian festivals but, until the sixteenth century, it was only one of many. Easter and Corpus Christi were considered to be just as important, and, indeed, better occasions for public celebrations.

For most people, social life was linked firmly to the Church. They met their friends' weekly, or even daily at the parish church. Religious plays and processions provided the main form of public entertainment: the theatre as we know it today grew out of such dramatic representations of stories from the Bible. And a fashionable preacher could attract a following that made him a very important person in the State.

The most remarkable of these preachers was a monk called Girolamo Savonarola. He was not a Florentine but a 'foreigner' — having been born in the city of Ferrara — but he made his mark in Florence almost immediately after arriving there in 1489. He was not a big man, but he was immensely impressive and people who saw and heard him never forgot him. The place where he preached was in the great cathedral and people in their thousands would crowd in to hear his burning sermons.

Savonarola believed that he had the gift of prophecy and had been given a divine mission first to reform Florence and then the world. He feared nobody, whether it was the Pope in Rome or the Medici in Florence, or the Florentines themselves. He told them they were evil, corrupt, doomed to Hell unless they mended their ways. He attacked the women for their vanity, the men for their lust for gold. And he succeeded, for a time at least, in reforming the Florentines. They threw off their beautiful clothes in favour of sober garments. They made a great bonfire in the Piazza della Signoria where they burnt all 'objects of vanity' — which included works of art as well as cosmetics and the like.

They even made him lord of their city after the death of Lorenzo. Savonarola believed — with justice — that it was wrong for one man to have such power and persuaded the Florentines to make Christ the King of Florence, with Savonarola as His regent.

It could not last, of course. The Florentines were human and, after their first burst of enthusiasm, they became tired of sermons and plain food, and began to long for the gay old days. At length Savonarola went too far in his attacks on the Pope and he was condemned to death. The Florentines themselves prepared the fire that was to burn him and, at the end, threw his ashes into the river. The Kingdom of Christ was over, and the Florentines turned again to the Medici family. But Lorenzo, too, was dead and his son was a weakling who had betrayed his city to an enemy. And when the Florentines did at last achieve freedom again, they found that the fatherly Medici had turned into tyrants. Lorenzo and Cosimo, who had done so much for their city, had been proud to call themselves citizens. The last Medici made themselves into Dukes and looked upon the ancient city of Florence as though it were their private property.

HOW DO WE KNOW?

Apart from the fact that the Florentine artists left such a vivid picture of their city, there are two main reasons why we know so much about what happened in the city nearly 500 years ago. The first is because the Florentines were tradesmen, and the second is because they must have been the biggest gossips the world has ever seen.

The ability to keep accounts is one of the most vital things a tradesman has to learn. In order to keep accounts he must be accurate and well informed. It is no accident that the Florentines were the first people in Italy to have a clear idea of the size of their population. While other cities were guessing wildly, and missing the mark by many thousands, the Florentines not only knew how many there were, but what they did for a living, what they ate, how much they earned.

All the guild officials kept careful records of their meetings. The government — which was composed of these same guild officials — did the same thing. Over many years, a tremendous number of records were compiled. Some of them were like the reports of our own parliamentary meetings in which speeches are reported at full length. Others were regulations to control various aspects of the city's life, or reports from ambassadors sent to other cities and countries.

These are the official records, and these alone would enable a historian to build up a clear picture. But there are two other kinds of records which, because they are unofficial, tell us not only what the Florentines were doing, but what they were thinking. These records are private letters and chronicles — the result of a Florentine gossiping with distant friends, or with himself.

A chronicle was simply a form of diary in which the writer jotted down details of what was happening in the city or elsewhere. Almost every Italian city could boast of at least one chronicler. In Florence, a merchant called Giovanni Villani began in 1300 to think about writing a chronicle that was to set a pattern for others to follow, so that by the time of the Medici there were several of these personal 'histories' written while history was being made. They vary a lot. Some of the writers give an almost day-by-day account, while others may jump weeks or even months between entries. They have to be used very carefully: the writer, after all, is only recording what he has heard in the city, and gossip is not always accurate. But the Florentine chroniclers did manage to be astonishingly well informed. Giovanni Villani, for instance, noted that cannon had been used in the battle of Crecy in distant France — the first time that the use of cannon had been recorded in Europe. And whether he is right or wrong, the chronicler's record is invaluable because it shows what he, a Florentine, thought was happening at the time, or what should happen.

During the time of old Cosimo de' Medici a bookseller by the name of Vespasiano da Bisticci began jotting down notes about the famous people of his time. The notes were eventually turned into a book called *The Lives of Illustrious Men* and in a modest foreword, Bisticci declared that though his talents were humble he believed that people who came afterwards would welcome even his unpolished attempts to record the actions of great men while they were still alive. In fact, Vespasiano was a very good writer, able to give us a vivid picture of a living, breathing man in a few words. He was in an excellent position not only to pick up gossip, but also to 'interview' his subjects almost as though he were a newspaper reporter, for his bookshop was famous throughout Italy and customers came to it even from distant England. He was immensely popular, being a gentle, good little man with a lively sense of curiosity but with malice towards nobody and many men who first came as customers returned as friends. Some of the men whose lives he recorded have long been forgotten, but others were to achieve lasting fame and it is fascinating to have a glimpse of these great figures before the world at large recognised them. Especially valuable is his picture of Cosimo de' Medici.

Bisticci's record is half way between the old-fashioned chronicle and modern biography. During the time of the Medici real history was being written — but it was being written with an eye to posterity. Far more interesting, because truly unselfconscious, were the letters written by contemporaries. A large number of Florentines were absent from their city for long periods:

some were artists working in Rome or London or Paris; some were merchants wandering all over the civilised world in search of trade. And to keep contact during their time away from home, they wrote endless letters to friends in the city. They passed on gossip about what was happening in the outside world and, in return, wanted information about what was happening in Florence. And what they learned we, too, can learn from the same letters.

A NOTE TO THE READER

If you have enjoyed this book enough to leave a review on **Amazon** and **Goodreads**, then we would be truly grateful.
The Estate of E. R. Chamberlin

Sapere Books is an exciting new publisher of brilliant fiction and popular history.

To find out more about our latest releases and our monthly bargain books visit our website:
saperebooks.com